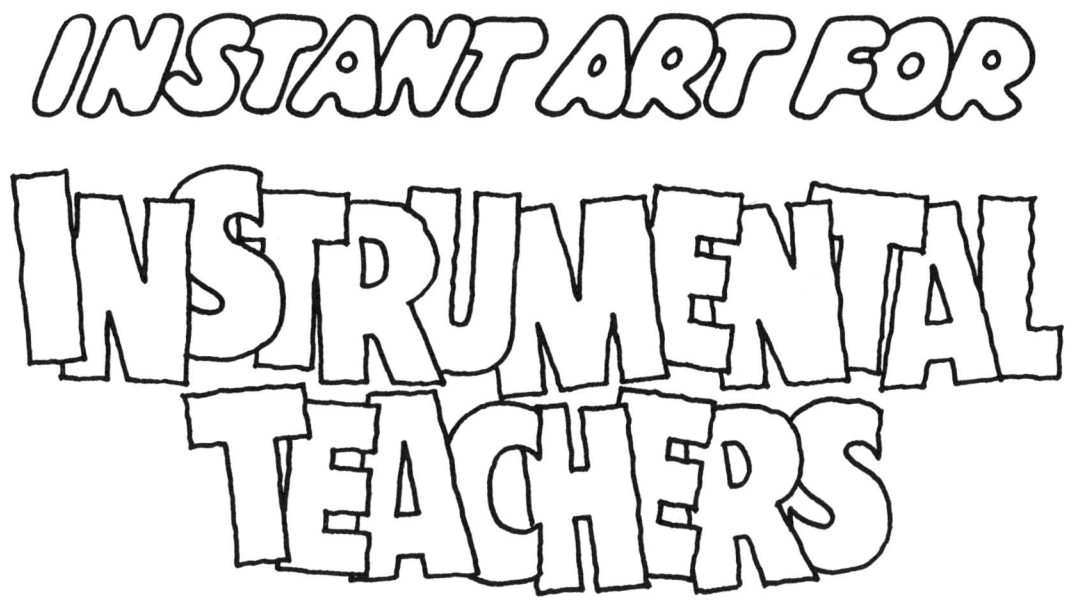

INSTANT ART FOR INSTRUMENTAL TEACHERS

by

Christopher Tambling

Kevin Mayhew

First published in 1996 by
KEVIN MAYHEW LTD
Rattlesden
Bury St Edmunds
Suffolk IP30 0SZ

ISBN 0 86209 824 6
Catalogue No 1396044

Cover illustration by Claire James
Cover design by Graham Johnstone and Veronica Ward

Illustrated by Neil Pinchbeck
Typesetting by Louise Hill
Music setting by Donald Thomson
Printed and bound in Great Britain

CONTENTS

USING THIS BOOK

Instant Art for Instrumental Teachers is a resource book with a variety of applications. It contains photocopiable worksheets intended primarily for the one-to-one music lesson, but could equally well be used in class situations. The worksheets are intended to be handed out at the end of a lesson, as a supplement to a pupil's music practice, but they could equally well be worked on by the pupil and teacher together during a lesson. The aim is to cover all of the requirements of the Grades 1 to 3 Theory exams in one book, and to provide useful background information about composers, musical instruments and other areas which might help in the development of a pupil's general musicianship.

NOTE THIS - 1

Here are the notes of the treble clef

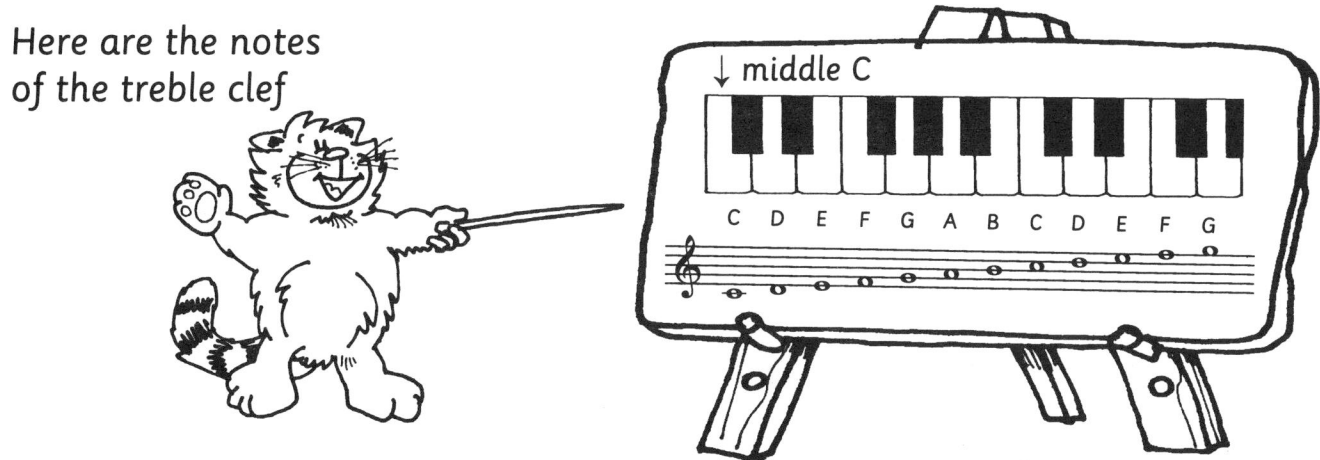

First of all, let's practise writing the treble clef

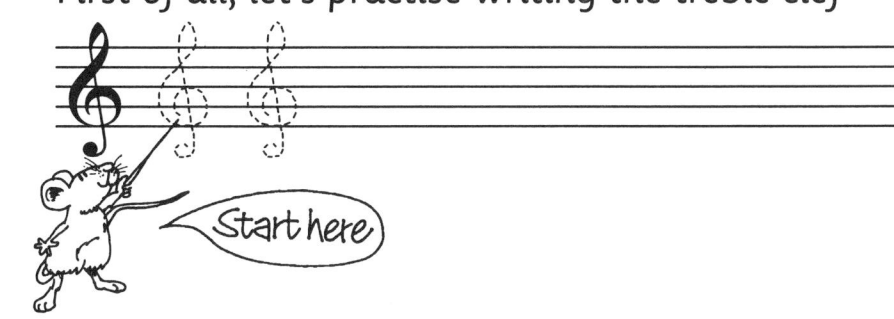

Here's how to remember the names of the notes
in the spaces . . .   on the lines . . .

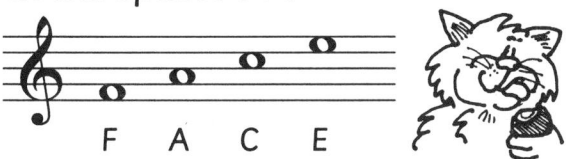   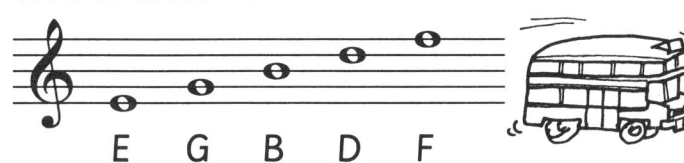

F A C E   E G B D F

FACE, or Felix Adores Chocolate Eggs   Every Green Bus Drives Fast

Can you think of any other ways to remember these letters?

NOTE QUIZ   Can you name these notes?

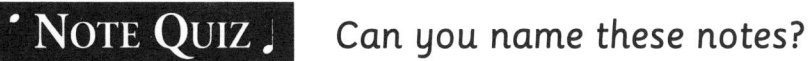

Can you write these notes?

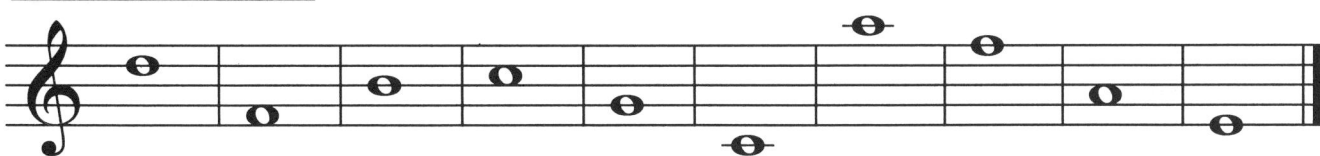

A   E   B   C   G   D   F   E   G   F

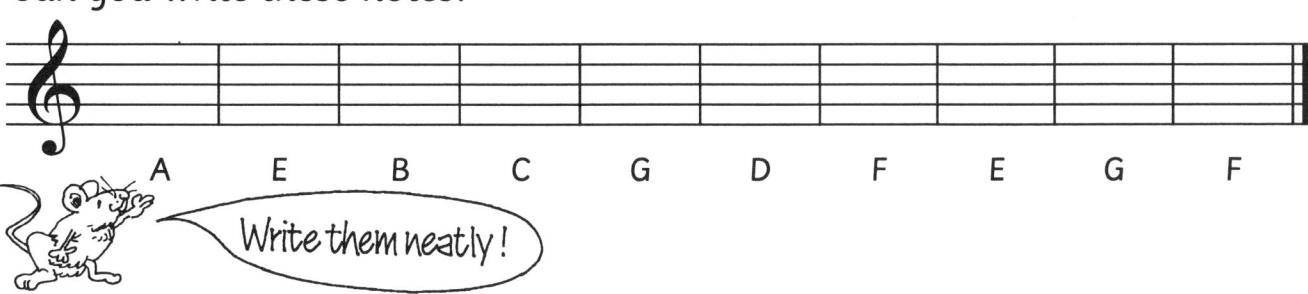

Write them neatly!

NOTE THIS - 2

Here are the notes
of the bass clef

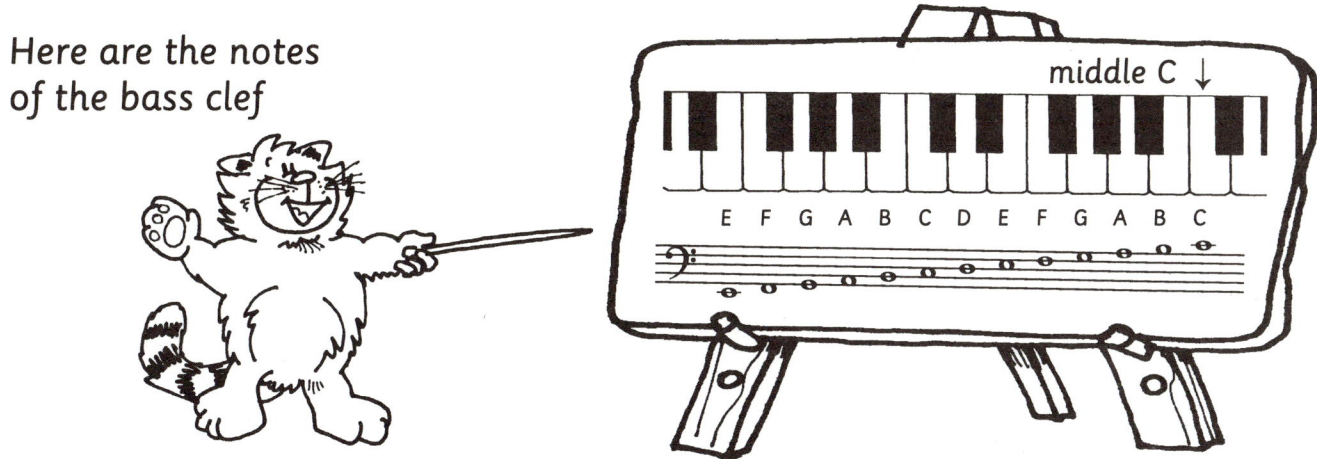

The bass clef is easy to draw. Have a go!

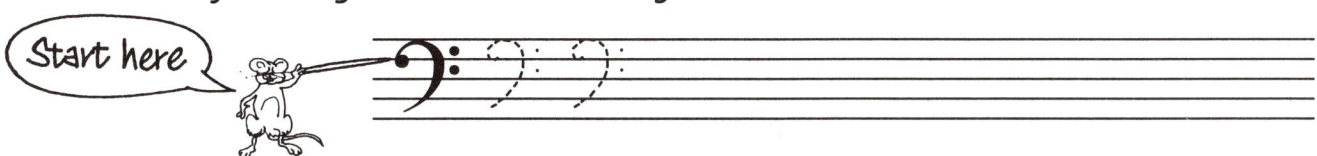

Here's a way of remembering the notes of the bass clef
in the spaces . . .   on the lines . . .

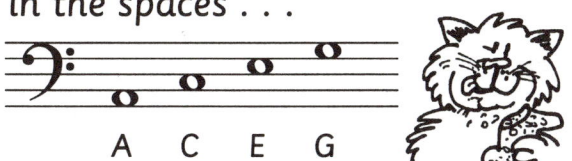

A C E G

All Cats Eat Gingerbread

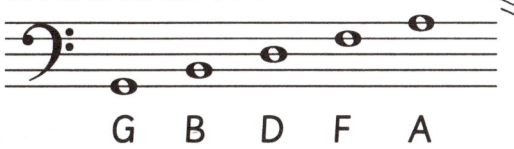

G B D F A

Green Buses Drive Fast Always

Now see if you can write these notes

A   E   B   C   G   D   F   E   G   F

Can you give the letter names of these notes?

𝄢 or 𝄞 ? What do you think?

Can you remember all of the notes on the bass clef and the treble clef? Lets see!

Now add the right clefs to make the letter name correct:

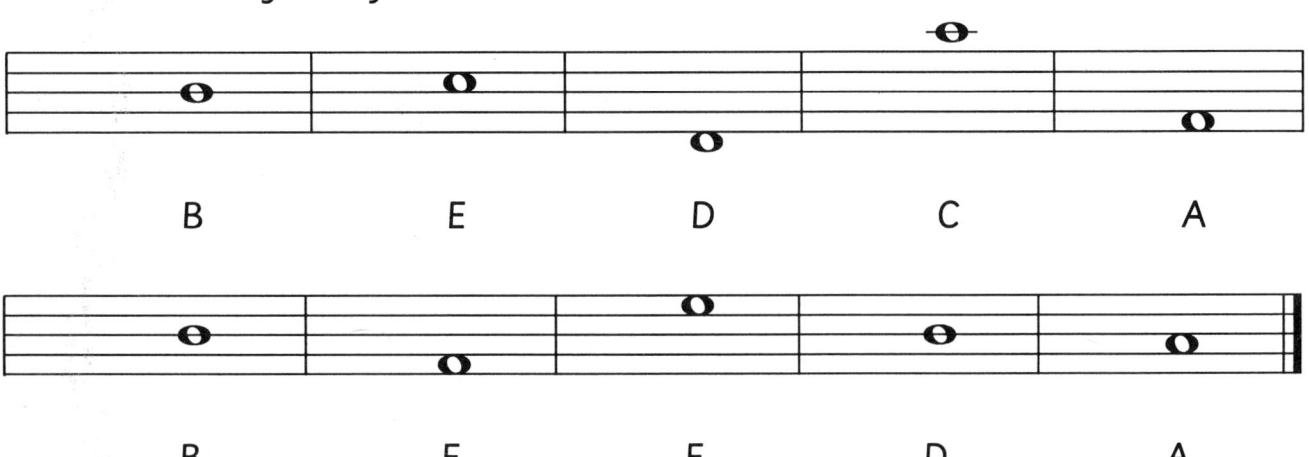

B   E   D   C   A

B   F   E   D   A

Unscramble the instrument names and match them up with their players.

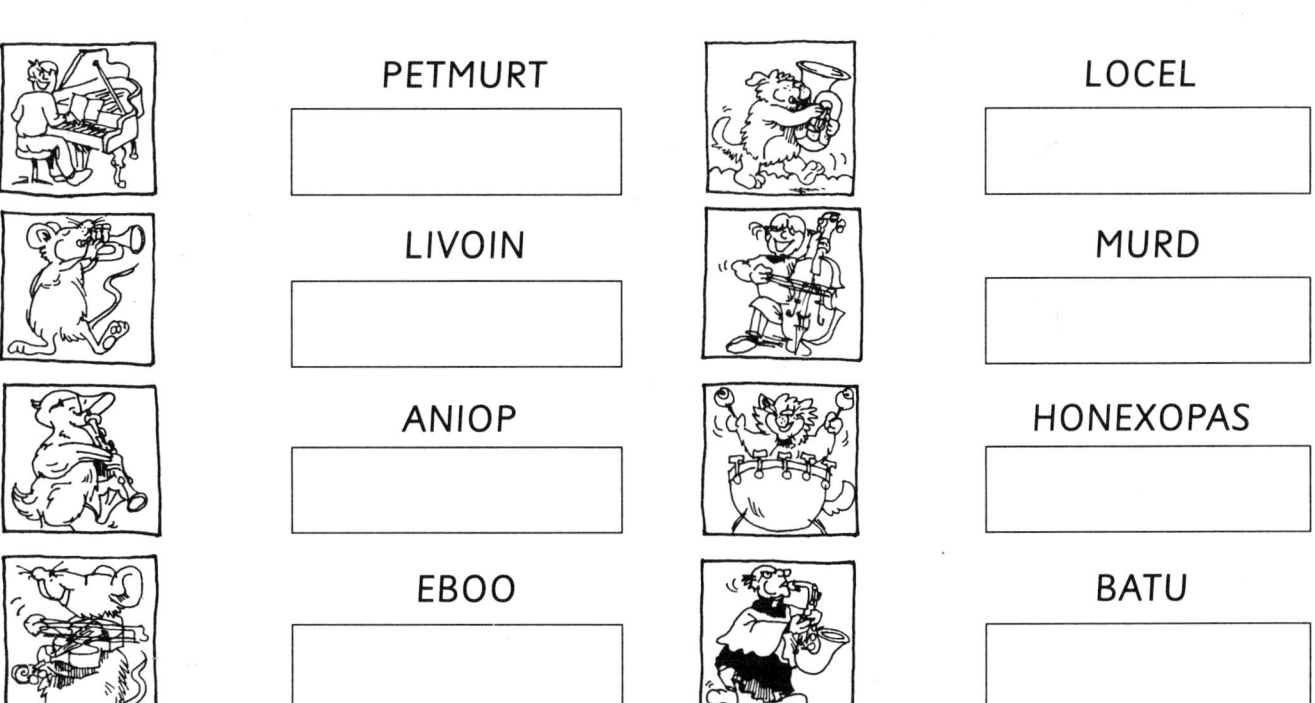

PETMURT

LIVOIN

ANIOP

EBOO

LOCEL

MURD

HONEXOPAS

BATU

MAJOR SCALES are made up of intervals of TONES and SEMITONES. Scales that go up are called ASCENDING scales: those that come down are DESCENDING.

This is C major ascending   Here is G major descending

These are Semitones   *This is a Key Signature*

Label these two scales

_____ major _____   _____ major _____

These key signatures are all muddled up. Can you match them up?

C major, bass clef	F major, treble clef
G major, treble clef	G major, bass clef
D major, treble clef	C major, treble clef
D major, bass clef	F major, bass clef

These tunes have been written without key signatures.
Can you write them out again, using the correct key signatures?

Write your key signature before the time signature.

MINER scales sound sadder than major scales.
There are two types of minor scale: HARMONIC
and MELODIC.

Play these pairs of scales through
– Can you spot the differences between them?
– Can you mark in the semitones?

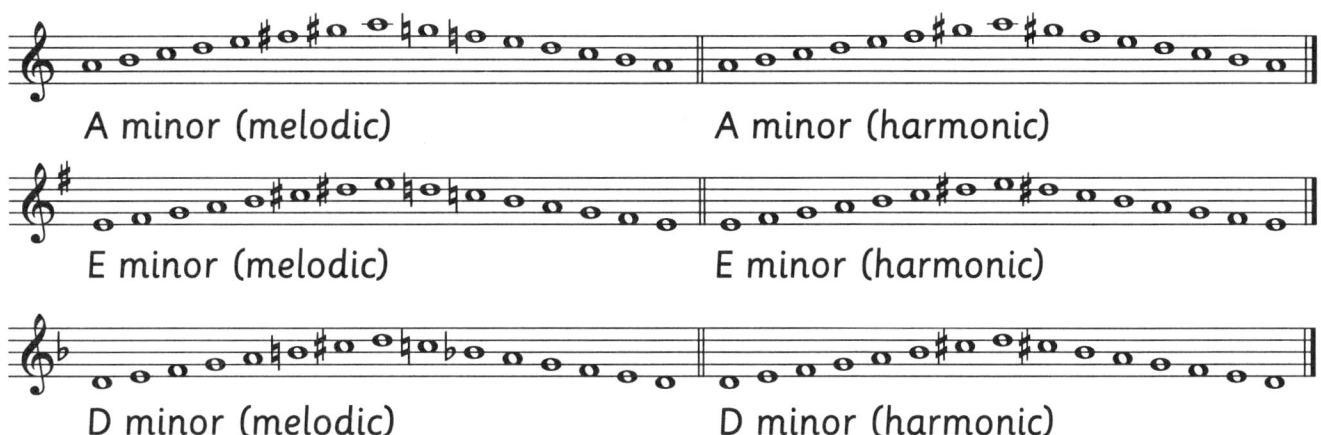

Each minor key has a RELATIVE MAJOR key. This is the major key that has
the same key signature. Can you complete these sentences?

____ major is the relative major of A minor
____ major is the relative major of D minor
____ major is the relative major of E minor

C major is the relative major of ____ minor
G major is the relative major of ____ minor
F major is the relative major of ____ minor

Hint! Look at the
3rd note of each
minor scale -this
will help you get
the right answer

Now write in the following key signatures:

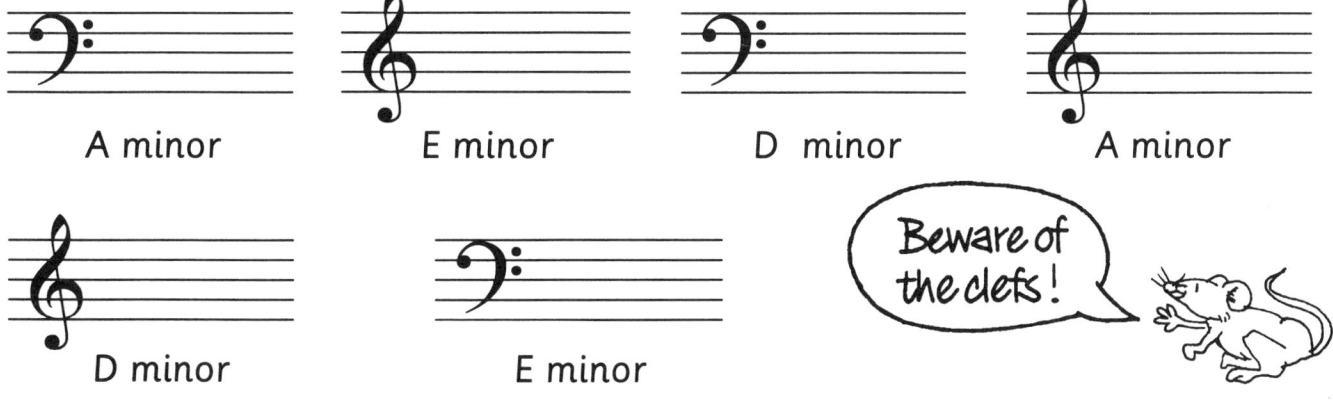

Beware of
the clefs!

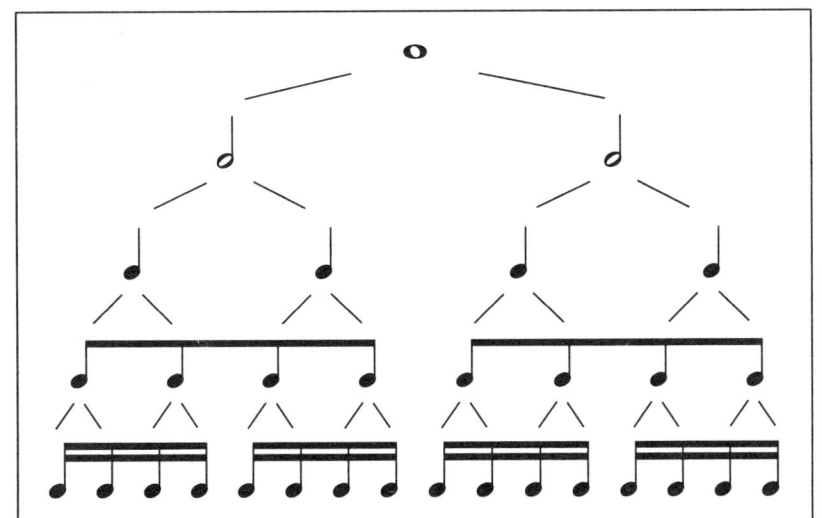

1 semibreve (Whole note)
. . . is equal to . . .
2 minims (1/2 notes)
. . . are equal to . . .
4 crotchets (1/4 notes)
. . . are equal to . . .
8 quavers (1/8 notes)
. . . are equal to . . .
16 semiquavers (1/16 notes)

Now try and clap the rhythm written above.
Can you write your own rhythm? Have a go!

Group these rhythms
correctly underneath

Fill in the missing notes
to make the bar complete

Placing a dot after a note makes it half as long again

For example

♩. = ♩ ♪

♩. = ♩ ♩

♪ NOTE QUIZ ♩

1. How many crotchets ♩ are there in a dotted minim ♩. ? _____

2. How many quavers ♪ are there in a dotted crotchet ♩. ? _____

3. How many semiquavers ♫ are there in a dotted quaver ♪. ? _____

4. How many semiquavers ♫ are there in a dotted minim ♩. ? _____

Don't confuse this with the Staccato dot ♩ which makes things shorter!

Can you add the missing dots in this tune?

Now make up a tune using dotted notes

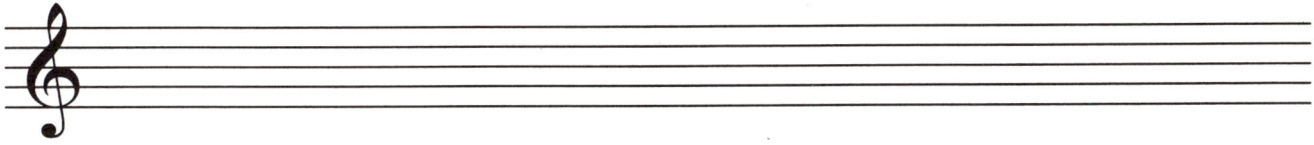

Good luck! Don't forget the time signature and key signature

TIME, PLEASE

At the start of each piece of music you
will find two numbers after the key signature.
These are known as the TIME SIGNATURE.
Here are some examples.

Duple (2) time	
$\frac{2}{4}$	$\frac{2}{2}$ or ¢

$\frac{2}{4}$ means there are two crotchets (1/4 notes) in each bar.

$\frac{2}{2}$ means there are two minims (1/2 notes) in each bar.

Triple (3) time	
$\frac{3}{4}$	$\frac{3}{2}$

What does $\frac{3}{4}$ mean? _____

What does $\frac{2}{2}$ mean? _____

Quadruple (4) time	
$\frac{4}{4}$ or c	$\frac{4}{2}$

Add the missing time signatures

Put in the missing barlines.

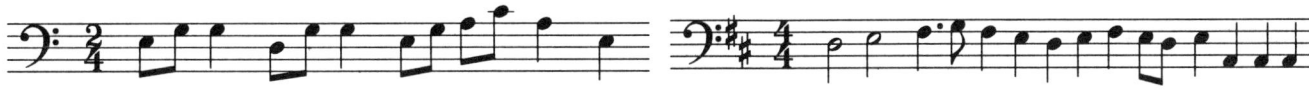

Antonio Vivaldi (1678-1741) was a priest and a musician who lived and worked in Venice, the great Italian city of canals, islands and churches. He was known as the 'red priest' because of the colour of his hair, but most of his working life was spent writing operas, concertos (over 500!) and other vocal and instrumental pieces. Many of his works were written for the musicians at a girls' orphanage in Venice, where he worked. Vivaldi is perhaps best known for his four descriptive violin concertos known as 'The Four Seasons'. For each concerto, Vivaldi provided a 'programme' to explain what he is describing in the music. He includes such detail as raindrops, a dog barking and hunting calls.

THINGS TO DO

Listen to a recording of 'The Four Seasons'.
Follow the 'programme' if you can.
How realistic is the musical depiction of what is going on?

Find the names of some of Vivaldi's pieces and the instruments he used in this wordsearch:

M	A	N	T	R	U	G	C	E	N	T	K
A	S	U	M	M	E	R	E	C	P	S	M
G	T	P	O	A	C	E	L	L	O	P	R
N	T	O	R	N	G	T	L	M	F	R	O
I	E	J	S	D	N	N	I	L	O	I	V
F	P	L	L	O	C	I	I	L	O	N	I
I	M	N	U	L	A	W	N	B	X	G	O
C	U	V	I	I	W	I	N	T	I	R	L
A	R	N	R	N	M	U	T	U	A	C	M
T	T	O	R	G	A	N	C	P	T	S	A
I	L	U	M	A	S	T	T	B	A	T	X
G	L	O	I	R	A	I	Q	Z	R	V	T

SPRING
SUMMER
AUTUMN
WINTER
MANDOLIN
VIOLIN

MAGNIFICAT
GLORIA
CELLO
ORGAN
TRUMPET

Look at this piece of music by Antonio Vivaldi –
play it if you can.
Then answer the questions underneath.

AUTUMN *by Vivaldi*

Allegro (♩ = 120)

1. What does **Allegro** mean? _____

2. What does (♩ = 120) signify? _____

3. Explain $\frac{4}{4}$ _____

4. What does *f* mean? _____

5. What is *p* short for? _____

6. What key is this piece in? _____

7. What degree of the scale does it start on? _____

8. What is the shortest note? _____

9. a) Which note is used most often in this extract? _____
   b) How often does it appear? _____

10. The notes in bar 9 have not been correctly grouped.
    Can you write the bar out correctly?

Don't forget to write
the treble clef and the
key signature

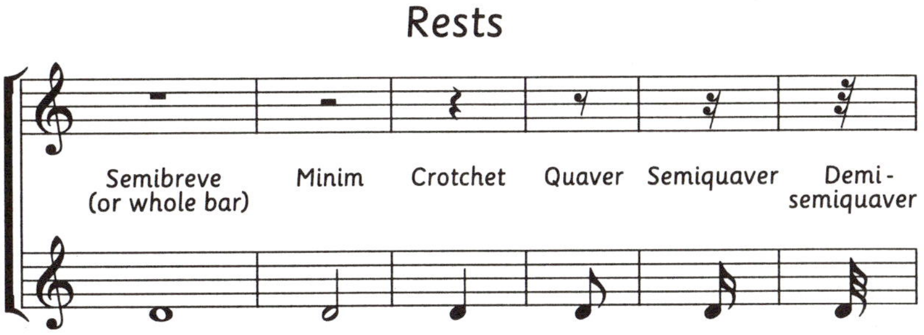

Rests

Add a rest or rests where there is an asterisk.
If you're not sure, look at the information above, or ask your teacher.

These useful terms and signs have been all mixed up. Can you link them up with their correct definitions?

cantabile	a little
pianissimo *pp*	majestically
accelerando	repeat marks
maestoso	octave
crescendo	in time
8va	very quiet
adagio	in a singing style
fine	get faster and faster
ritardando	the end
grave	slow down gradually
dolce	slow and solemn
allegro	fast
a tempo	get louder and louder
‖: :‖	go back to the start
poco	slow
da capo	sweetly

HIGH NOTES AND LOW NOTES Worksheet 13

LEGER lines are used for notes too high or too low for the stave.
Fill in the missing notes.

Make sure your leger lines are all on the same level

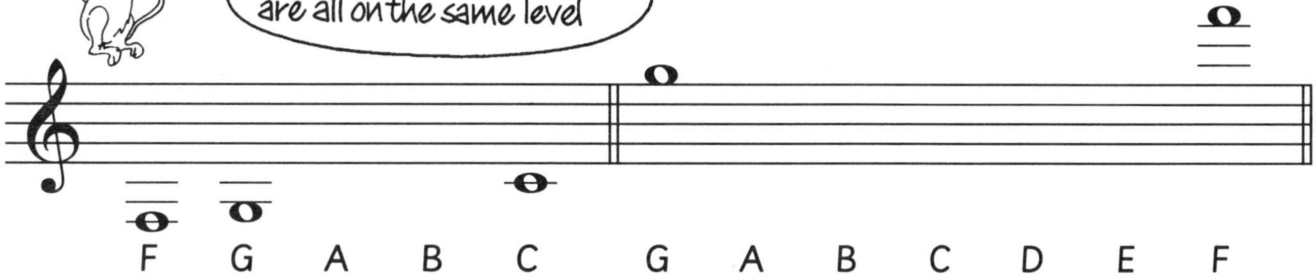

F G A B C G A B C D E F

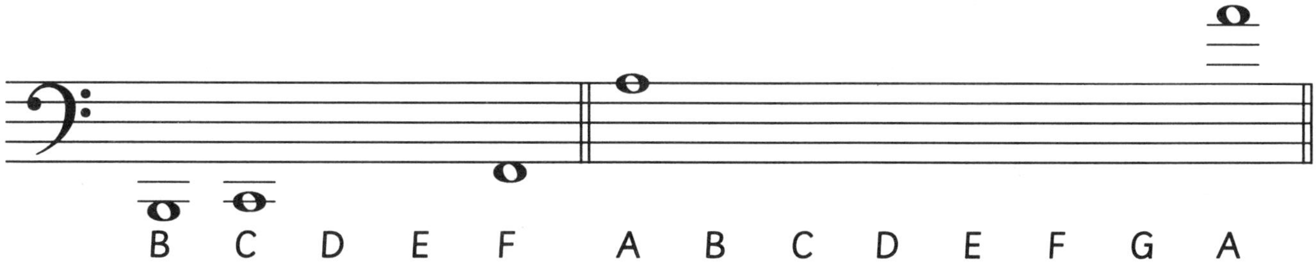

B C D E F A B C D E F G A

Can you name these notes?

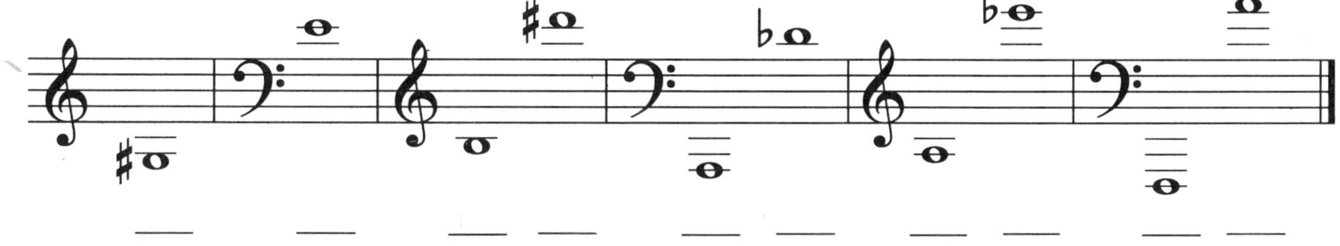

Write this melody out in the treble clef, at the same pitch.

Now it's your turn to compose a tune!
Try improvising a melody on your instrument
and then writing it down.
Here are a few hints.

Slurs and phrase marks help too

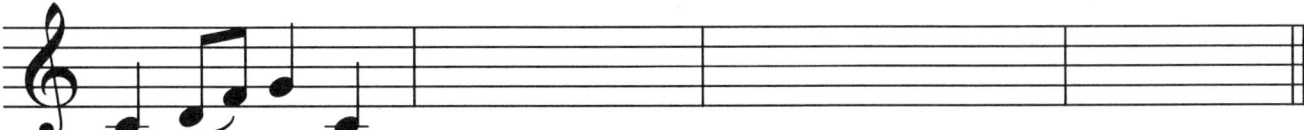

mf   *cresc.*   *f*

First choose a clef and key. Don't forget the time signature

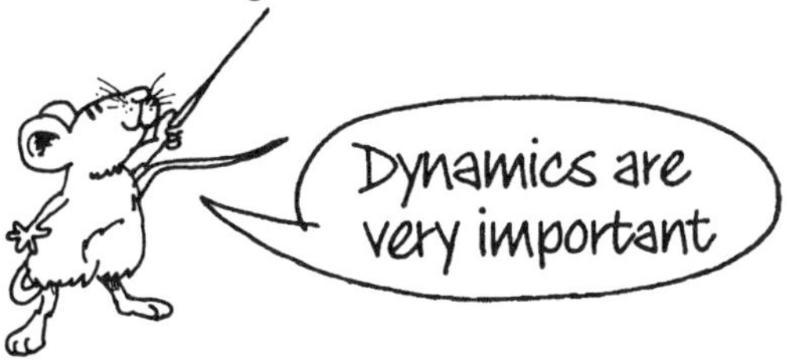

Dynamics are very important

Try writing a four bar melody using the opening given below.
Don't be afraid of repeating notes, bars or rhythms – make it interesting!

Now try writing one of your own.
You could even extend it to 8 or 16 bars if you are feeling adventurous . . .

TRIPLETS!

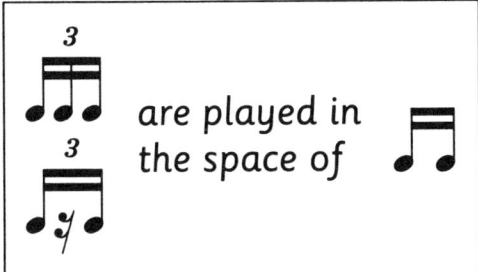 are played in the space of

Triplet rhythms, like dotted rhythms, make your music sound even more interesting.

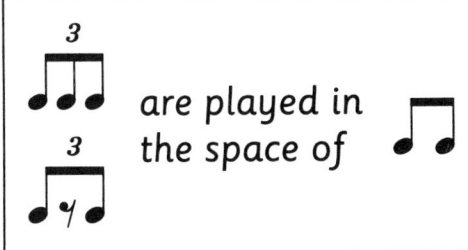 are played in the space of

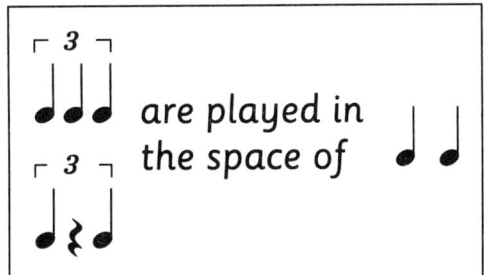 are played in the space of

Can you fill in the missing barlines?

Fill in the missing triplet signs

Now write a tune using triplets. Here is the first bar:

During his lifetime George Frideric Handel (1685-1759) was one of Europe's leading musical figures. He travelled widely and first became well known as a composer of OPERA.

Though he was German by birth Handel spent the latter part of his life in England. Here he wrote a series of ORATORIOS – his best loved work is undoubtedly the 'Messiah'.

Besides vocal and choral works Handel wrote many small instrumental pieces, as well as large works for massed orchestral forces such as the 'Music for the Royal Fireworks' and the 'Water Music' suite.

THINGS TO DO

Can you find out the names of two other composers born in the same year as Handel?

Can you discover how Handel managed to become a musician, against the wishes of his father?

Crack this code to find out. **CODEBREAKER**

LOOKING FOR CLUES-2   Worksheet 17

Look at this extract from Handel's 'Water Music'.
Play it then answer the questions underneath.

AIR from WATER MUSIC *by Handel*

1. What does **Presto** mean? _____

2. What key is this piece in? _____

3. a) What do the initials *mf* stand for? _____
   b) What do they mean? _____
   c) What does *cresc.* mean? _____

4. What degree of the scale does this extract end on? _____

5. a) What is the shortest note used? _____
   b) How often does it appear? _____

6. What do the ⌒ signs mean? _____

7. What does *tr* signify? _____

8. What happens when you see the :‖ sign? _____

9. Can you think of any instruments in the orchestra that might be able to play this tune? _____

10. Write out bars 5-8 an octave lower, in the bass clef.

Semiquavers ($^1/_{16}$ notes) can be divided in half to give demisemiquavers ($^1/_{32}$ notes)

Rests: semiquaver = ♪
        demisemiquaver = ♪

NOTE QUIZ ♩

1. How many demisemiquavers are there in a crotchet? _____

2. How many semiquavers are there in a minim? _____

3. How many demisemiquavers are there in a quarter? _____

4. How many demisemiquavers are there in a dotted quaver? _____

Can you add the missing rests in these tunes?

Now add the missing barlines!
(The two tunes begin on the
first beat of the bar)

Hint! Remember that notes are grouped in beats

Some melodies start before the first beat
of the first bar.
A note before the opening bar is known as
an 'up beat' or an 'anacrusis'.

Here are two examples:

Note that the last bar
has been shortened to
make up for the 'up beat'

Can you make up four-bar rhythms using these openings?
(Write them on one note, or make up a melody)

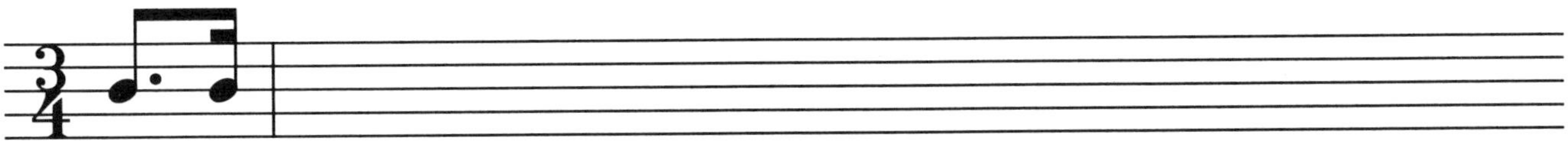

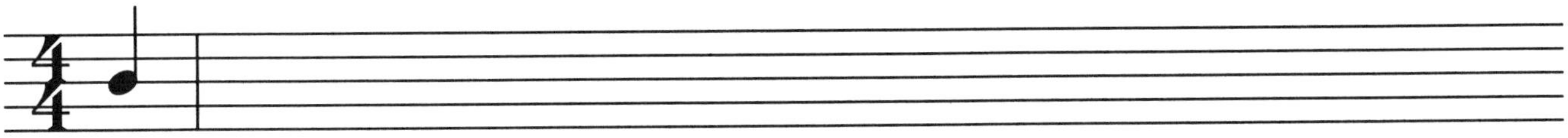

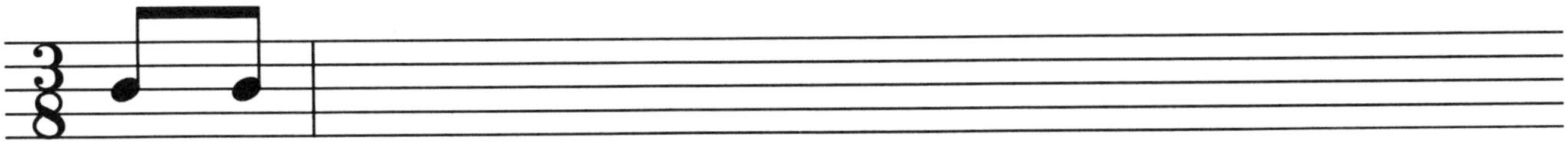

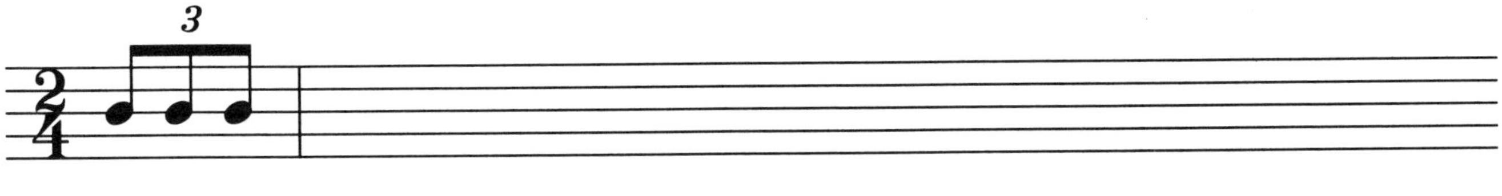

I'VE LOST MY MUSIC

Can you help these famous composers find their music?
Each composer has lost two pieces.

Ludwig van
Beethoven

Felix
Mendelssohn

Wolfgang Amadeus
Mozart

Johann
Strauss

Peter Ilyich
Tchaikovsky

George Frideric
Handel

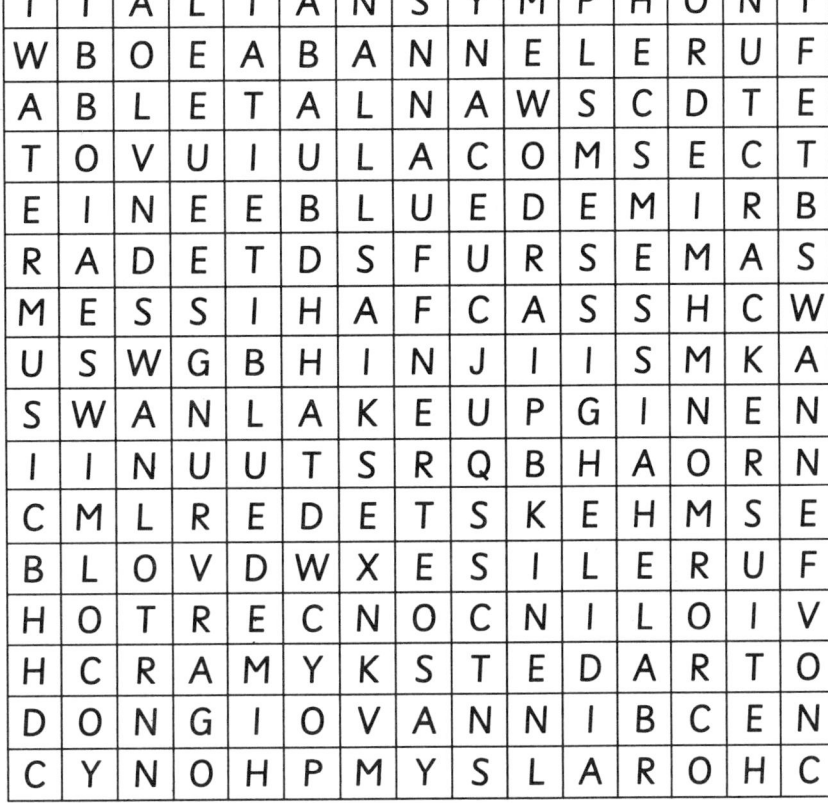

I	T	A	L	I	A	N	S	Y	M	P	H	O	N	Y
W	B	O	E	A	B	A	N	N	E	L	E	R	U	F
A	B	L	E	T	A	L	N	A	W	S	C	D	T	E
T	O	V	U	I	U	L	A	C	O	M	S	E	C	T
E	I	N	E	E	B	L	U	E	D	E	M	I	R	B
R	A	D	E	T	D	S	F	U	R	S	E	M	A	S
M	E	S	S	I	H	A	F	C	A	S	S	H	C	W
U	S	W	G	B	H	I	N	J	I	I	S	M	K	A
S	W	A	N	L	A	K	E	U	P	G	I	N	E	N
I	I	N	U	U	T	S	R	Q	B	H	A	O	R	N
C	M	L	R	E	D	E	T	S	K	E	H	M	S	E
B	L	O	V	D	W	X	E	S	I	L	E	R	U	F
H	O	T	R	E	C	N	O	C	N	I	L	O	I	V
H	C	R	A	M	Y	K	S	T	E	D	A	R	T	O
D	O	N	G	I	O	V	A	N	N	I	B	C	E	N
C	Y	N	O	H	P	M	Y	S	L	A	R	O	H	C

BLUE DANUBE — Strauss
CHORAL SYMPHONY — Beethoven
DON GIOVANNI — Mozart
FÜR ELISE — Beethoven
ITALIAN SYMPHONY — Mendelssohn
MAGIC FLUTE — Mozart
MESSIAH — Handel
NUTCRACKER SUITE — Tchaikovsky
RADETSKY MARCH — Strauss
SWAN LAKE — Tchaikovsky
VIOLIN CONCERTO — Beethoven
WATER MUSIC — Handel

Here's how to harmonise a melody using some basic CHORDS.

Chords are made up of the 1st, 3rd and 5th degrees of the scale played together.

Try playing these chords on the keyboard with your left hand.

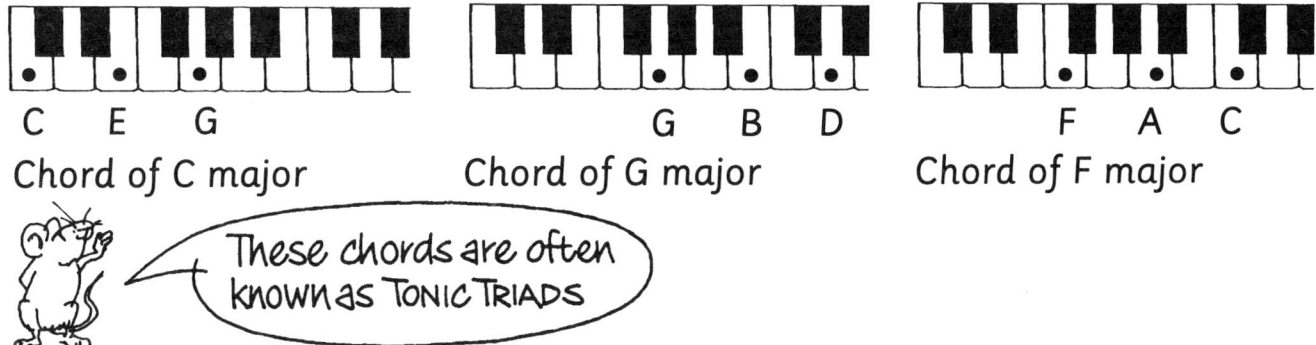

C   E   G   G   B   D   F   A   C

Chord of C major   Chord of G major   Chord of F major

These chords are often known as TONIC TRIADS

Try playing these tunes with your right hand, and the chords indicated with your left hand.

LIGHTLY ROW

C   F   G   C   C   F   G   C   G   C

G   C   C   F   G   C   G   C

MY BONNY LIES OVER THE OCEAN

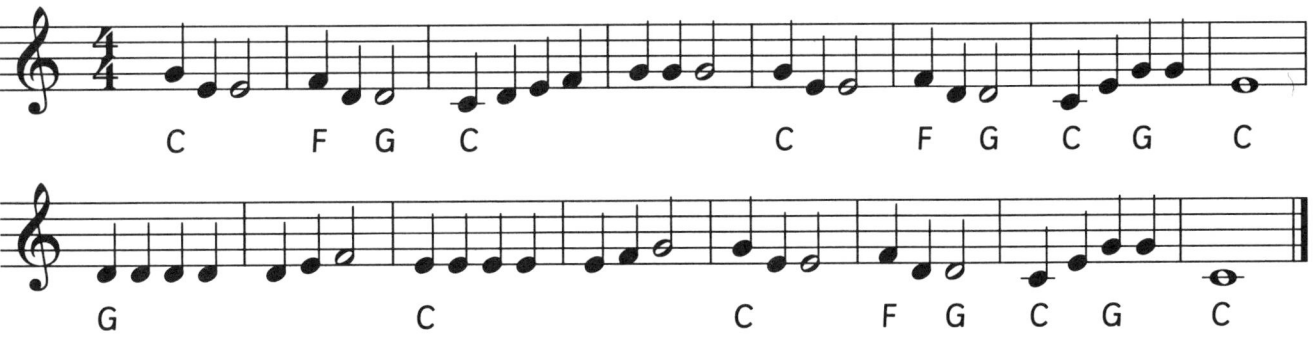

–   C   F   C   C   G

C   F   C   F   G   C

If you're feeling really brave try making up an 'oom pah pah' accompaniment

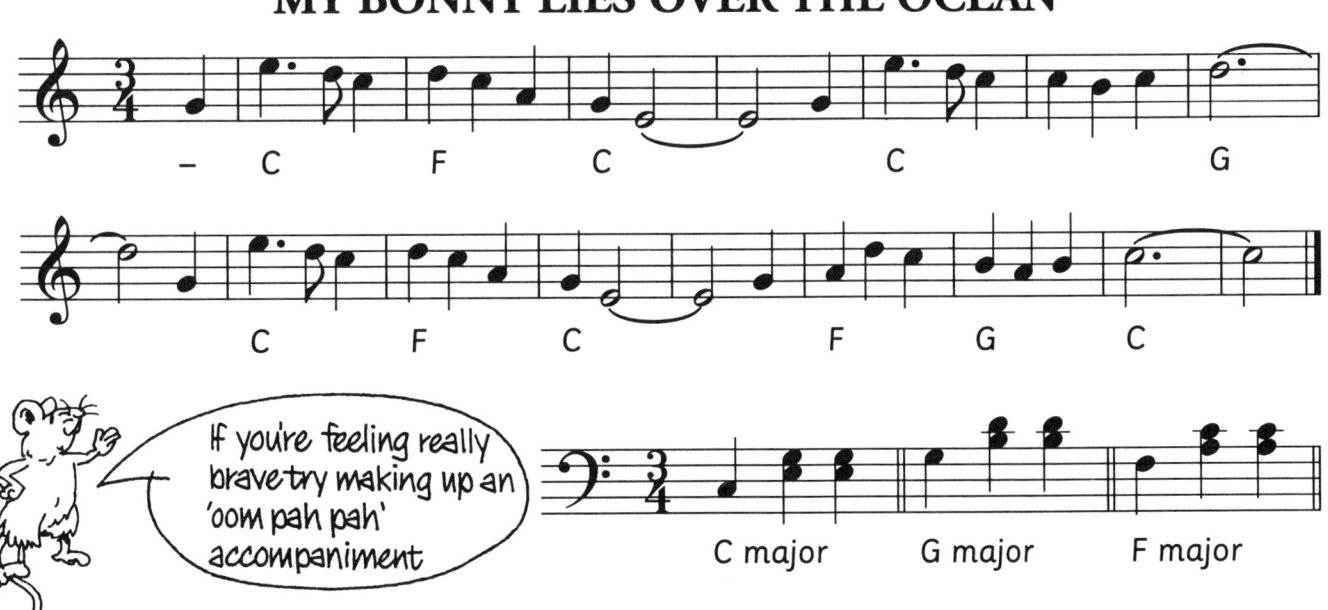

C major   G major   F major

What do these musical terms mean?
Can you link them up with their
correct definitions?

alla marcia	forced, accented
marcato	get gradually softer
rubato	lightly
grazioso	held back
energico	in time
senza	rather slow
delicato	lovingly
vivo	freedom of timing
forza	emphatically
amoroso	suddenly
sf or sfz	energetic
diminuendo	in the style of a march
adagietto	quick
legato	calmly
subito	gracefully
ritenuto	without
leggiero	delicately
tranquillo	force
a tempo	smoothly

Harmonising a tune at the keyboard isn't <u>too</u> difficult! Play this melody on the piano or keyboard, and see if you can choose the most suitable chord for the left hand (the accompaniment) from the chord bank. Write the letter names of the chords in the boxes like this: ☐C

LITTLE BROWN JUG

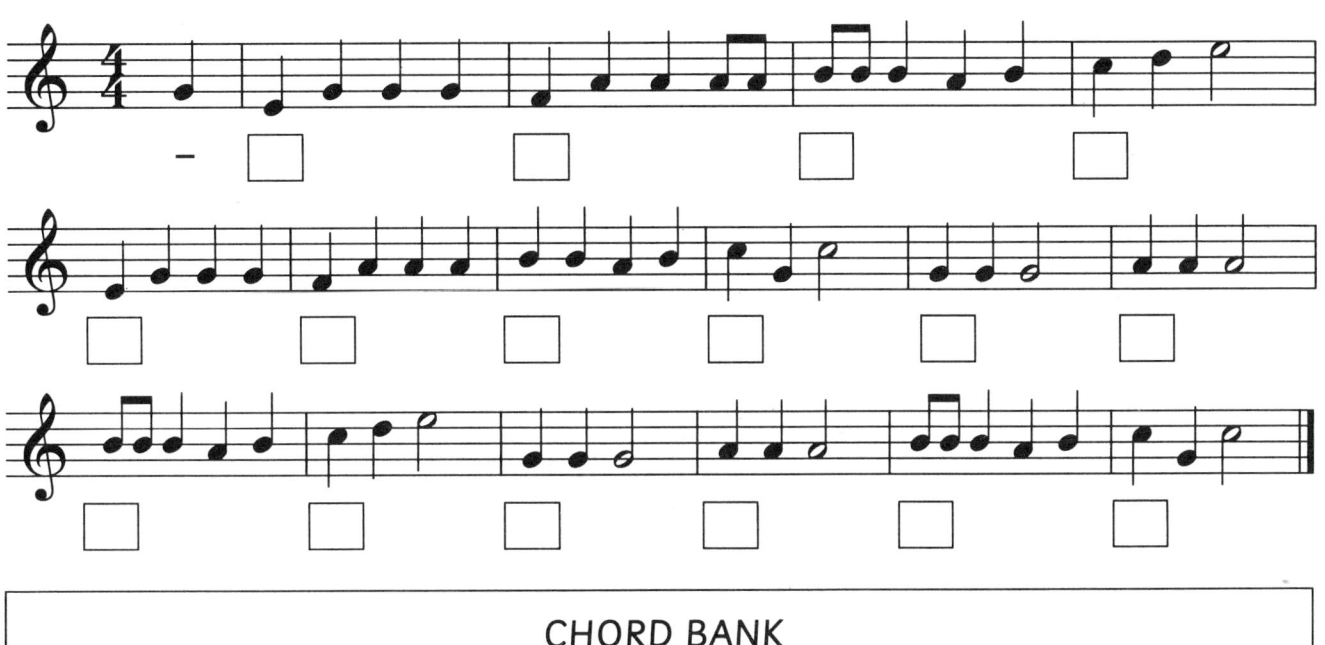

CHORD BANK

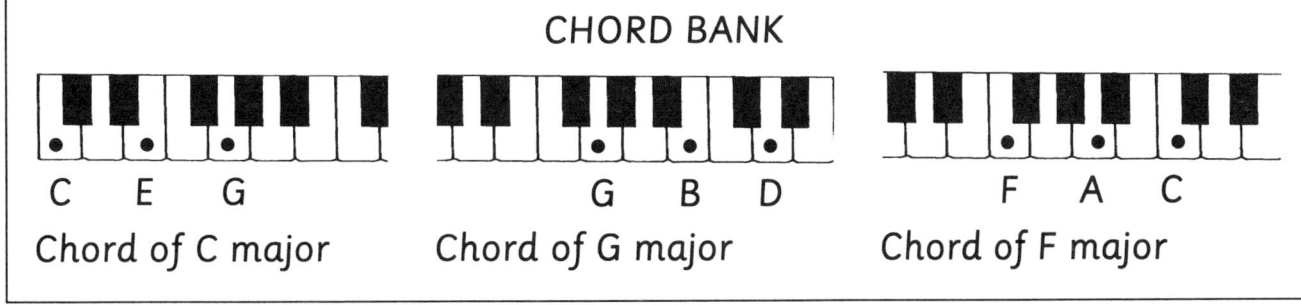

C E G	G B D	F A C
Chord of C major	Chord of G major	Chord of F major

You could even try making this tune more interesting by playing an 'oom pah oom pah' rhythm: instead of playing single chords

Try other chords if you like

 play

Oom pah oom pah!

Remember – you might find this easy, but practice makes 'purrfect'

Oh, no!

Here is some more information about key signatures. Look at the boxes carefully: in SIMPLE time the beats can be divided in half but in COMPOUND time they can be divided in three.

Duple (2) time

Simple

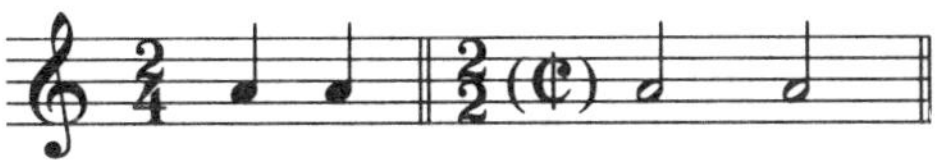

Compound

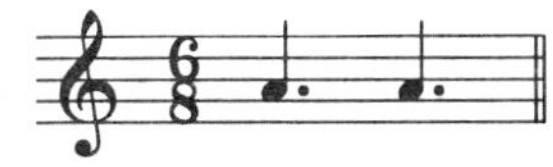

Triple (3) time

Simple

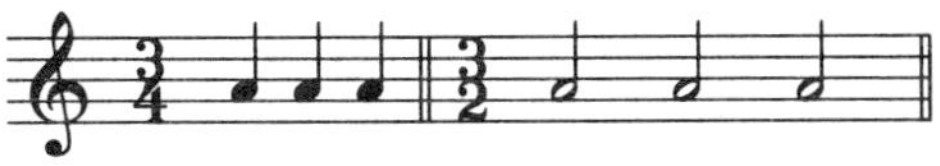

Compound

Quadruple (4) time

Simple

Compound

Here is an example of $\frac{6}{8}$ (compound duple time).

Notes are grouped in beats

Count 1   2   1   2   1   2   1   2

Can you put in the missing barlines?

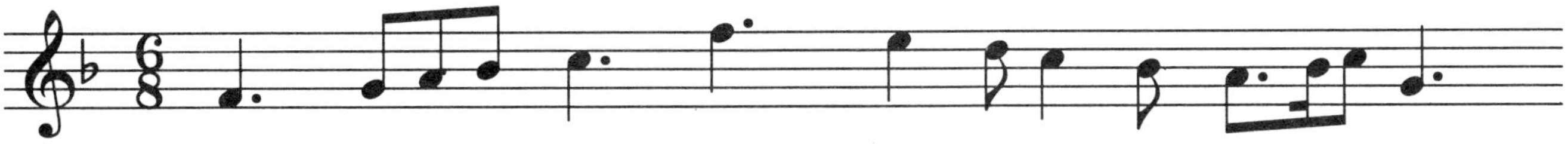

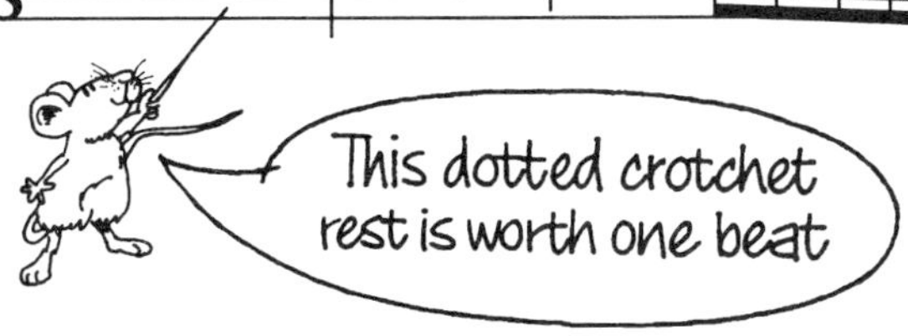

This dotted crotchet rest is worth one beat

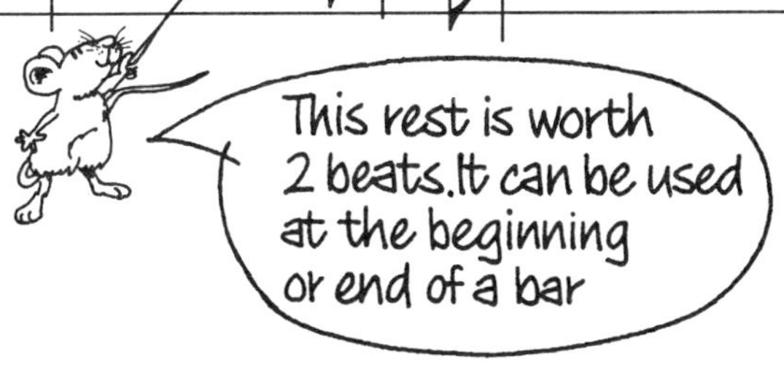

This rest is worth 2 beats. It can be used at the beginning or end of a bar

Can you fill in the missing rest or rests?

Johann Sebastian Bach (1685-1750) was a brilliant keyboard player who wrote many works for the organ and harpsichord. He was employed by various courts and churches throughout his life, and produced a wide variety of new music for many different occasions. As cantor of St Thomas' Church in Leipzig, he wrote many great choral works, including the magnificent 'St Matthew Passion'. His orchestral works include the six 'Brandenburg Concertos' – lively, energetic music enjoyed by players and audience alike.

THINGS TO DO

Can you find out what a concerto is?

Listen to Bach's Brandenburg Concerto No 2.

This piece features a number of solo instruments – can you tell which ones they are?

Unscramble these sentences to find out a bit more about this great composer.

As a young NAM, _____ Bach DELRATVEL _____

over 200 SMILE _____ on TOOF _____ to hear the famous

GARONIST _____ Buxtehude.

Bach OMCOPSED _____ a set of 48 ERLUPEDS _____

and GUFEUS _____ for the CHORDISPRAH. _____

MERBUNS _____ fascinated Bach. His <u>third</u> GRUBNEDNARB

_____ concerto uses <u>three</u> NOVILIS, _____ <u>three</u>

LOVIAS _____ and <u>three</u> LECLOS _____ (as well as <u>one</u>

BLEDOU SABS). _____

Look at this piece of music by Johann Sebastian Bach – play it then answer the questions underneath.

CONCERTO IN D MINOR FOR 2 VIOLINS *by Bach*

Largo ma non tanto

mf

1. What key is this extract in? _____

2. Can you explain what $\frac{12}{8}$ means? _____

3. What does **Largo ma non tanto** mean? _____

4. In the second bar, what is the difference between the ⌣

    and the ⌢ ? _____

5. What is the shortest note in this extract? _____

6. What does *mf* mean? _____

7. Can you write out the first bar, an octave lower, in the bass clef?

This chart will help you understand
INTERVALS in music.
Play the intervals through several times
and listen to the difference between them.

Here are the intervals in a major key (all related to the key-note).

| Major 2nd | Major 3rd | Perfect 4th | Perfect 5th | Major 6th | Major 7th | Perfect Octave |

In a minor key, you will meet other intervals –

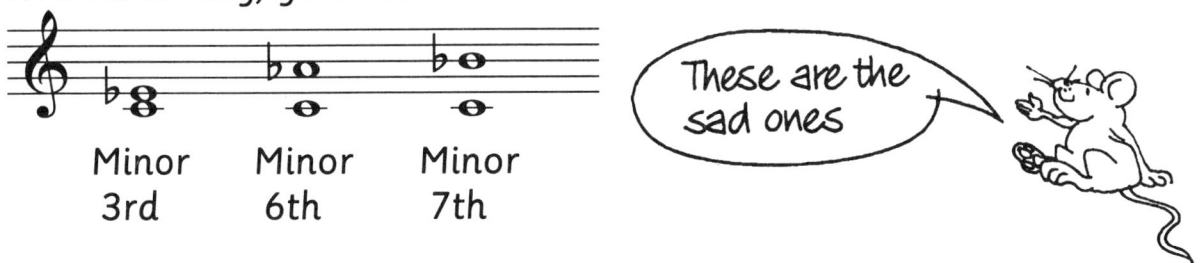

| Minor 3rd | Minor 6th | Minor 7th |

These are the sad ones

Can you work out what these intervals are?
The lowest note in each case is the key-note.

Major keys

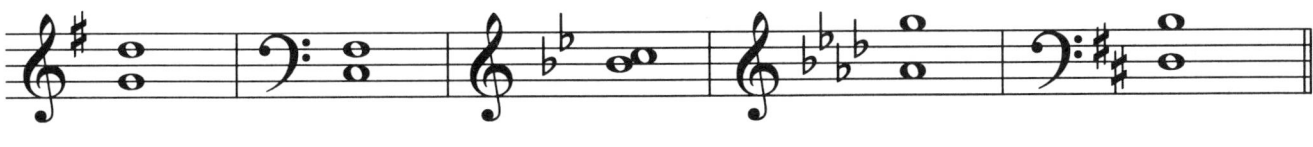

_____ _____ _____ _____ _____

Minor keys

_____ _____ _____ _____ _____

WHAT KEY?

This chart will help you learn the key signatures for all major and minor keys.

Sharp keys – go up a perfect 5th each time

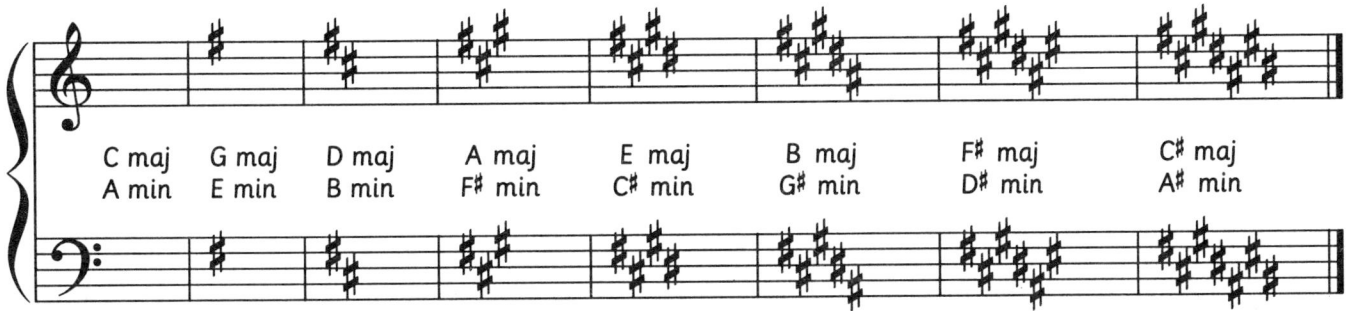

| C maj | G maj | D maj | A maj | E maj | B maj | F# maj | C# maj |
| A min | E min | B min | F# min | C# min | G# min | D# min | A# min |

Flat keys – go up a perfect 4th each time

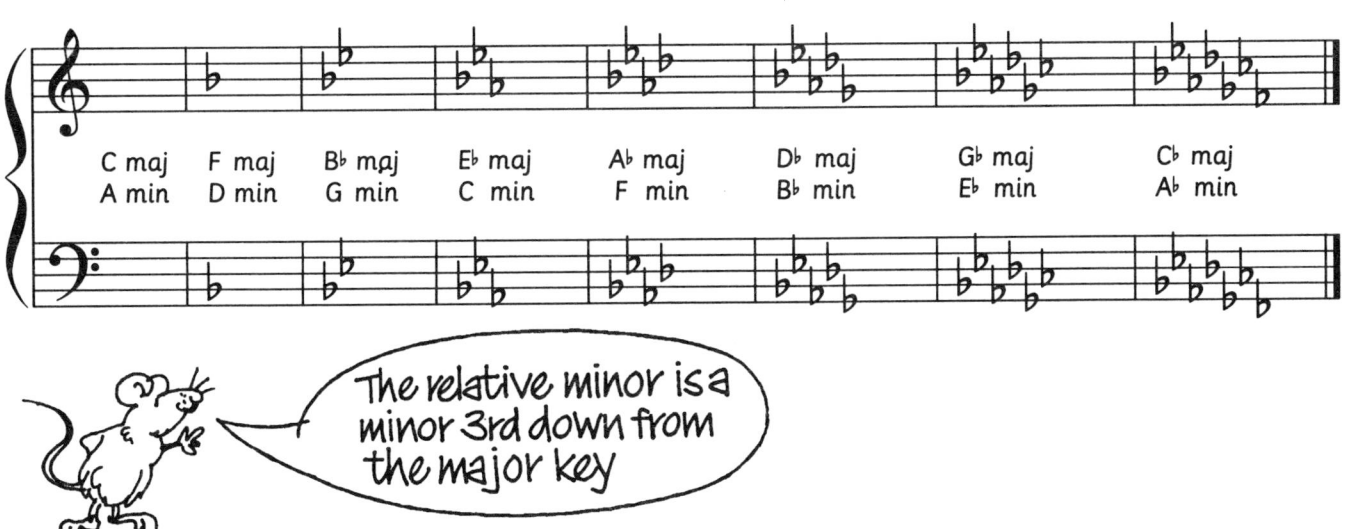

| C maj | F maj | B♭ maj | E♭ maj | A♭ maj | D♭ maj | G♭ maj | C♭ maj |
| A min | D min | G min | C min | F min | B♭ min | E♭ min | A♭ min |

The relative minor is a minor 3rd down from the major key

Learn this off by heart, so that you can remember the order of sharps in the key signature:

Fat Cats Get Dozy After Eating Beans

The order of flats is the same as this, only in reverse.

WHERE'S MY INSTRUMENT?   **Worksheet 29**

Victor has lost his Viola.
Can you help him find it?

Amazing!

Way in

What do these musical terms mean?
Can you link them up with their correct definitions?

molto pesante	rather slow
espressivo	broadening out
agitato	animated
lento	with vigour
animato	merrily
con brio	not too much
larghetto	in the same way
largamente	moderately quiet
non troppo	$\frac{2}{2}$ (¢) time
sempre fortissimo	playfully
allargando	very heavily
scherzando	sadly
simile	more
alla breve	slowly
giocoso	agitated
stringendo	always very loud
più	expressively
semplice	broadly
tristamente	getting gradually faster
mezzo piano	simply

Wolfgang Amadeus Mozart (1756-1791) began composing when he was only three years old. He was a highly talented child and travelled all over Europe with his father, giving breathtaking concert performances. He is perhaps best known for his operas such as 'The Magic Flute' and 'The Marriage of Figaro'. He found time to write 41 symphonies and a large number of instrumental, vocal and choral works. He died when he was only 35; his 'Requiem', said to have been commissioned by a mysterious stranger, was left unfinished at his death. It was later completed by his pupil Süssmayr.

One of Mozart's best loved compositions is the serenade 'Eine Kleine Nachtmusik'. Play through this excerpt from the first movement.

EINE KLEINE NACHTMUSIK *by Mozart*

THINGS TO DO

Can you find the right chords to accompany the melody from bar 5 onwards? Choose your chord from the Chord Bank and fill in the empty boxes.

CHORD BANK

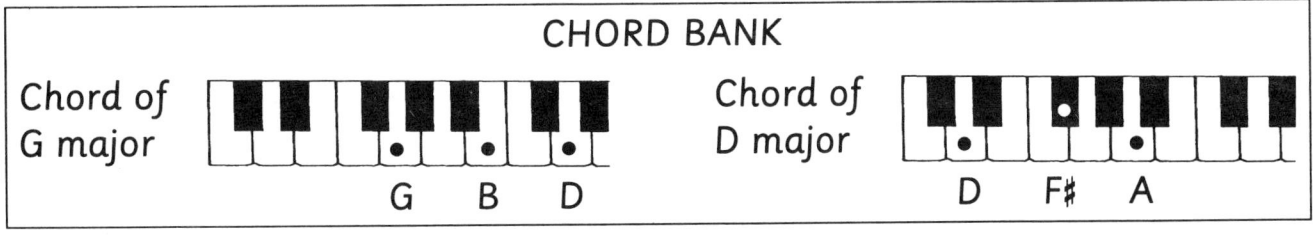

Chord of G major — G B D

Chord of D major — D F♯ A

Look at this piece of music by Mozart – play it through then answer the questions underneath.

DIES IRAE from 'REQUIEM' *by Mozart*

Allegro assai

Careful! look at the C♯s

1. What key is this extract in? _____

2. Explain the time signature. _____

   Is this compound or simple time? _____

   Duple, triple or quadruple? _____

3. What degree of the scale is the first note? _____

4. What is the interval between the first two notes? _____

5. Can you explain what the 𝄻 means in bar 2? _____

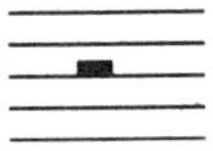

6. Name any two bars which have the same rhythm _____

7. Draw a circle round three notes which together make up a tonic triad.

8. What does *f* mean? _____

9. Can you transpose bars 4-8 down an octave, and into the bass clef?

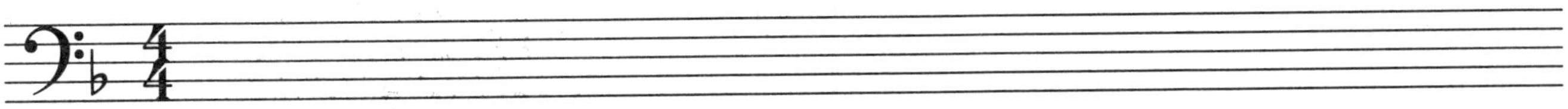

10. What does **Allegro assai** mean? _____

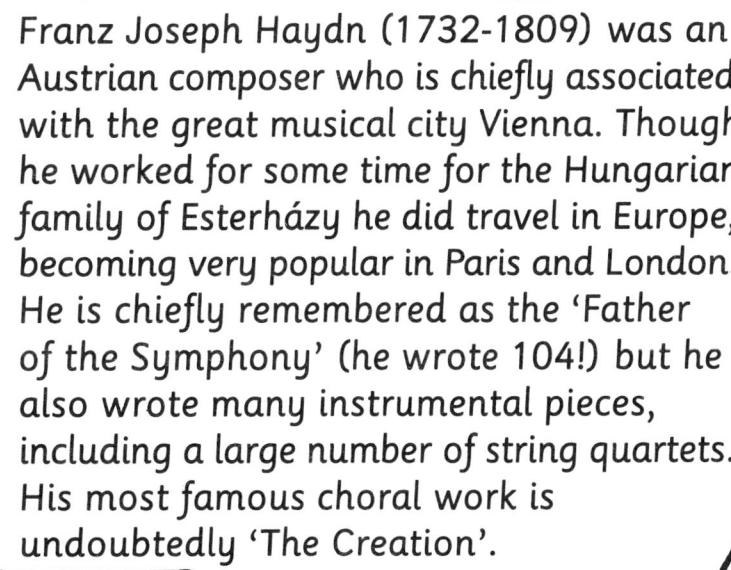

Franz Joseph Haydn (1732-1809) was an Austrian composer who is chiefly associated with the great musical city Vienna. Though he worked for some time for the Hungarian family of Esterházy he did travel in Europe, becoming very popular in Paris and London. He is chiefly remembered as the 'Father of the Symphony' (he wrote 104!) but he also wrote many instrumental pieces, including a large number of string quartets. His most famous choral work is undoubtedly 'The Creation'.

THINGS TO DO

Haydn had a great sense of humour. Listen to the second movement of his 'Surprise' Symphony (no. 94). Why do you think it has this nickname?

Play through this excerpt from the 'Surprise' Symphony.
Can you find the right chords to fit in the boxes?

SURPRISE SYMPHONY *by Haydn*

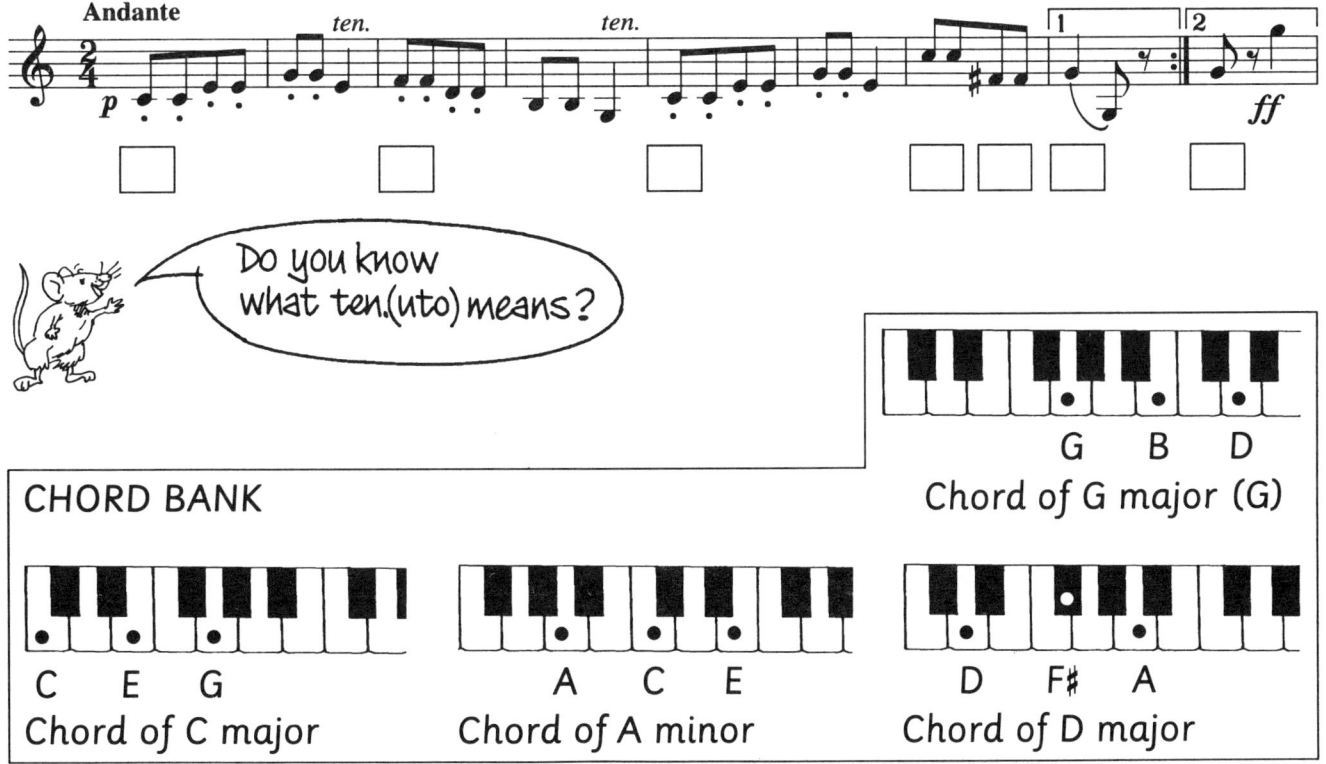

Play through this melody (often known as the 'Emperor's Hymn') by Haydn.
Then answer the questions beneath.

2ND MOVEMENT of 'EMPEROR' QUARTET *by Haydn*

1. What key is this piece in? _____

2. Can you explain **C** ? _____

3. What does **Poco adagio** mean? _____

4. Can you say what *p dolce* means? _____

5. What degree of the scale does the melody start on? _____

6. What is the interval between the 3rd and 4th notes in bar 2? _____

7. Draw a circle around three notes that make up a D major triad.

8. What does ⌢ mean in bar 8? _____

9. Name any two bars which have the same rhythm _____

10. Can you transpose the first line of music down an octave, but still in the treble clef?

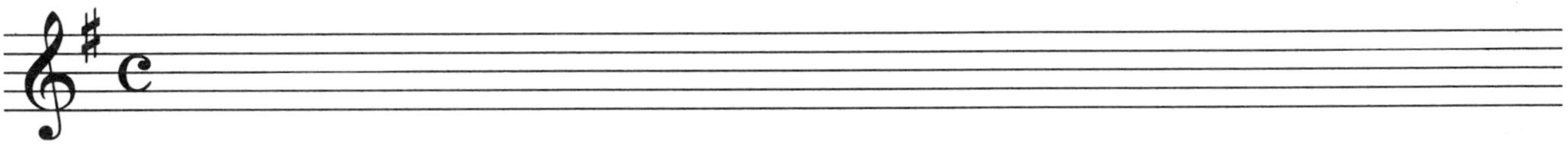

It's often useful to be able to transpose a melody up or down an octave, or to transpose it for a Bb instrument such as a clarinet or trumpet.

Here are some practice exercises for you.
Transpose this melody down an octave, into the bass clef.

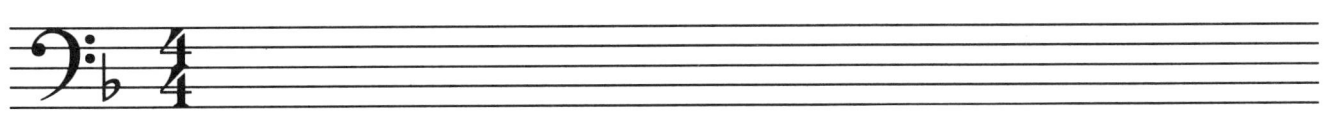

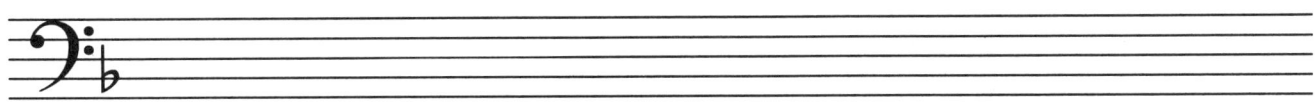

Bb instruments are called transposing instruments: their music is written a TONE (major 2nd) higher than usual.

WRITTEN   SOUNDS

Transpose this violin melody up a tone, for clarinet or trumpet.

5   1   2   3   4

Hint! write in the degrees of the scale and transfer these to the new key

Don't forget the new key signature

etc.

COMPOSER FILE: BEETHOVEN   Worksheet 36

Ludwig van Beethoven (1770-1827) is one of the giants of musical history. He was an abrupt, stubborn man, whose music reflects the passions and struggles of his life. Despite increasing deafness, he wrote nine symphonies, five piano concertos and a violin concerto, as well as many other instrumental pieces. His 32 piano sonatas include the well known 'Moonlight' and 'Pathétique' sonatas. Beethoven's 9th symphony is known as the 'Choral Symphony': at its conclusion, a choir and soloist sing the famous 'Ode to Joy'.

THINGS TO DO

Find out the titles of other works by Beethoven.

Play this extract from the 'Ode to Joy'.
Can you add appropriate dynamic marks, slurs and phrasing?

Try to add chords to it.

Play this extract from the slow movement
of Beethoven's 'Pathétique' sonata for piano.
Then answer the questions below.

PATHÉTIQUE SONATA *by Beethoven*

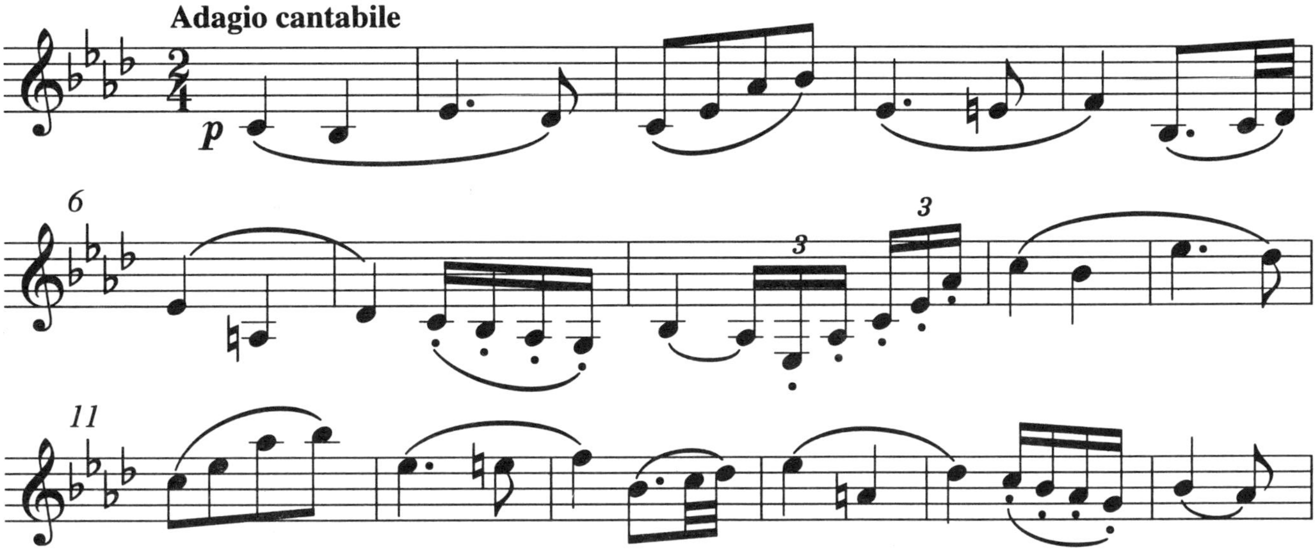

Adagio cantabile

1. What key is this piece in? _____

2. Explain what is meant by $\frac{2}{4}$ _____

3. Do you know what **Adagio cantabile** means? _____

4. What degree of the scale does the piece start on? _____

5. Circle three notes in a row which make up a triad of A♭ major.

6. What does the *3* mean over the semiquavers in bar 8? _____

7. What is the difference between bars 1-7 and bars 9-15? _____

_____

8. What is the interval between the last two notes? _____

9. What is the shortest note length in this extract? _____

10. What do the ⌣•⌣•⌣ signs mean? _____

HUNT THE COMPOSER

Can you find the names of fifteen famous composers in this wordsearch?

V	I	V	A	L	D	N	E	V	O	H	T	E	E	B
E	E	L	G	E	R	O	H	A	N	D	E	L	O	I
R	O	R	M	E	N	D	E	L	S	S	O	H	N	D
H	A	Y	D	I	N	T	H	O	O	B	A	R	K	L
D	V	E	R	I	D	C	K	R	N	I	R	S	T	A
I	C	L	B	R	A	H	M	S	D	P	H	A	E	V
R	P	G	R	B	E	A	T	E	Y	R	T	A	M	I
S	M	A	I	L	L	I	W	N	A	H	G	U	A	V
T	B	R	T	L	I	K	N	G	H	H	A	Y	Z	W
R	A	R	T	S	M	O	Z	A	R	T	G	L	A	N
A	A	V	E	R	D	V	I	V	A	N	O	T	R	L
U	M	O	N	O	C	S	C	H	U	B	E	R	T	O
S	C	H	U	B	E	K	H	A	N	D	L	E	L	L
S	T	R	O	W	S	Y	E	G	T	R	A	Z	O	M

BACH
BEETHOVEN
BRAHMS
BRITTEN
ELGAR
HANDEL
HAYDN
MENDELSSOHN

MOZART
SCHUBERT
STRAUSS
TCHAIKOVSKY
VAUGHAN WILLIAMS
VERDI
VIVALDI

Have fun

What do these musical terms and signs mean?
Can you link them up with their correct definitions?

allegretto		get gradually softer
mesto		first time
sostenuto		boldly
ritmico		extra staccato/detached
andantino		less movement
decrescendo		with feeling
tempo commodo		in a military style
fp		sustained
risoluto		fairly quick
con anima		well
ꞈ ꞈ		at a convenient pace
meno mosso		rhythmically
ben		with determination
>		faster walking pace
marziale		lively
vivace		sadly
primo volta		accent
deciso		loud then soft straight away

Felix Mendelssohn (1809-1847) was born in Hamburg in Germany and began composing at a very early age. He became a very popular figure in 19th century musical circles and travelled all over Europe as a conductor and performer: his overture, 'Fingal's Cave' (The Hebrides) was inspired by a visit to Scotland. His many compositions include piano and chamber works, five symphonies, a violin concerto and many orchestral and choral works.

FINGAL'S CAVE *by Mendelssohn*

THINGS TO DO

Listen to 'Fingal's Cave'. The piece has been described as a 'musical seascape'. What does the composer do to create a picture with this music?

Rearrange the mixed up letters to discover more about Mendelssohn.

Mendelssohn wrote the Overture to A DUMSERMIM TINGHS RAMED

_____ when he was only

TENVENSEE _____ years old.

EQUEN TICVARIO _____ liked Mendelssohn's music very much.

Mendelssohn wrote many SNOGS HOTUWIT ROWDS _____

_____ for the piano.

Here is the start of the famous 'Wedding March' from Mendelssohn's 'A Midsummer Night's Dream'.
Play it if you can, then answer the questions underneath.

WEDDING MARCH *by Mendelssohn*

1. What does **Allegro vivace** mean? _____

2. What key is this piece in? _____

3. Can you explain the following terms and signs?
   cresc. (bar 4) _____
   ff (bar 6) _____
   sf (bar 10) _____

4. What instruments in the orchestra
   might play the opening fanfare? _____

5. What degree of the scale does bar 7 start on? _____

6. In which bar is there an arpeggio of C major? _____

7. a) What is the longest note used in this extract? _____
   b) How often does it appear? _____

8. Write out the first five bars, an octave lower in the bass clef.

Now let's see how much music theory
you can remember.

1. Add the correct time signature and barlines.

2. Now add rests and an appropriate time signature.

3. a) Write the key signature and tonic triad of C♯ minor and also the scale
   of C♯ melodic minor ascending.

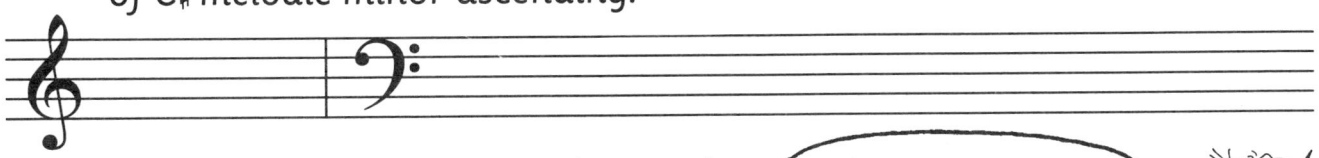

tonic triad   ascending scale   Watch the clefs!

b) Now do the same for A♭ major.

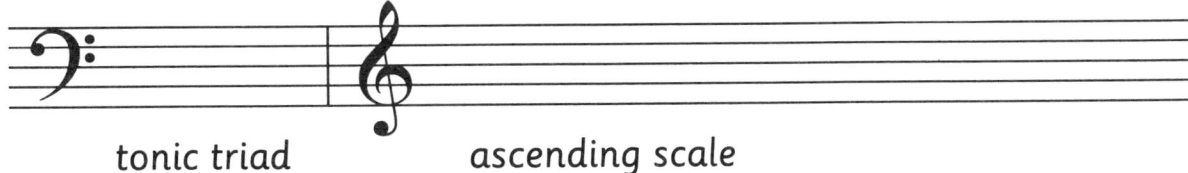

tonic triad   ascending scale

4. Time to compose! Write a four-bar rhythm in $\frac{6}{8}$. Begin and end as shown.

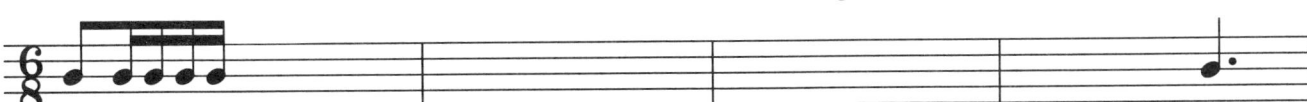

5. Transpose this violin melody down an octave for the cello.

Here is an extract from Beethoven's
'Pastoral Symphony'.
Can you answer the questions below?

PASTORAL SYMPHONY *by Beethoven*

1. What key is this piece in? _____

2. Can you add the time signature? _____

3. What does **Allegretto** mean? _____

4. What is the interval between the highest note and the lowest note
   in the extract? _____

5. What is the interval between the last two notes? _____

6. Circle three notes following each other which make up a tonic triad.

7. Explain: ⌒ (bar 1) _____

   ⌒ (bar 4) _____

   p (bar 1) _____

8. Transpose bars 7 and 8 down an octave into the bass clef.
   The first note has been done for you.

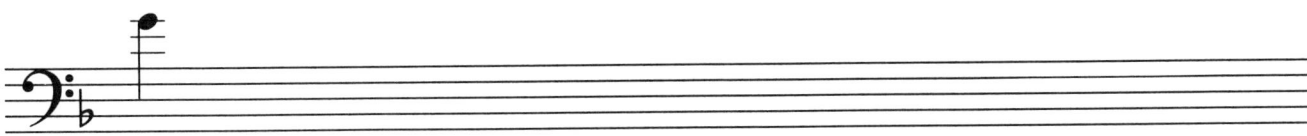

GUITAR CHORD BANK

TUNING YOUR GUITAR

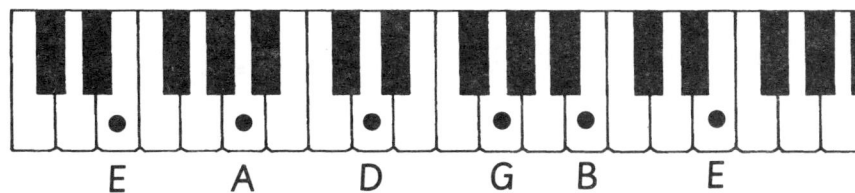

Middle C ↓

E   A   D   G   B   E

The first string on the guitar is E
The second string is A
The third string is D
The fourth string is G
The fifth string is B
The sixth string is E

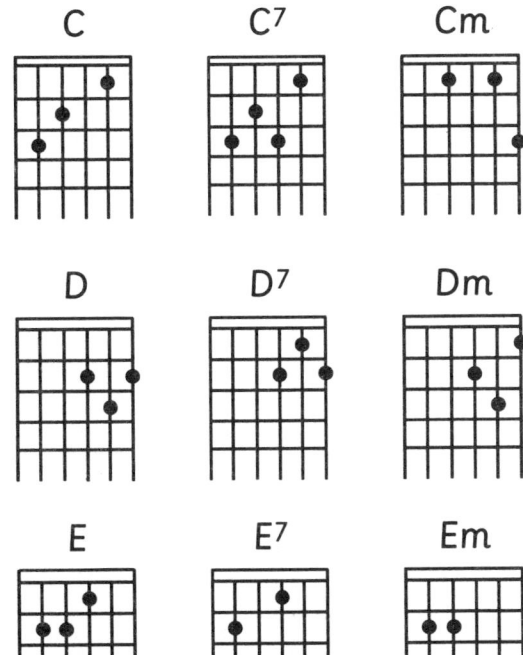

C   C⁷   Cm   F

D   D⁷   Dm   G   G⁷

E   E⁷   Em   A   A⁷   Am

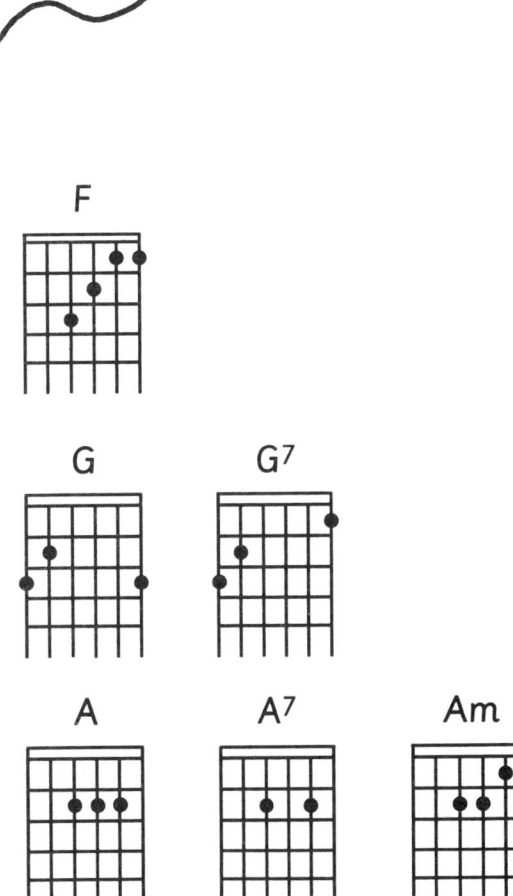

PRACTICE RECORD

Name _____

Term _____

Date	Teacher's Notes	✓	Mon	Tue	Wed	Thu	Fri	Sat	Sun
		Scales							
		Pieces							
		Scales							
		Pieces							
		Scales							
		Pieces							
		Scales							
		Pieces							
		Scales							
		Pieces							
		Scales							
		Pieces							
		Scales							
		Pieces							
		Scales							
		Pieces							
		Scales							
		Pieces							

MANUSCRIPT PAPER